The quoted ideas expressed in this book (but not Scripture verses) are not, in all cases, exact quotations, as some have been edited for clarity and brevity. In all cases, the author has attempted to maintain the speaker's original intent. In some cases, quoted material for this book was obtained from secondary sources, primarily print media. While every effort was made to ensure the accuracy of these sources, the accuracy cannot be guaranteed. For additions, deletions, corrections, or clarifications in future editions of this text, please write Freeman-Smith.

Scripture quotations are taken from:

The Holy Bible, King James Version (KJV)

The Holy Bible, New International Version (NIV) Copyright © 1973, 1978, 1984, by International Bible Society. Used by permission of Zondervan Publishing House. All rights reserved.

The Holy Bible, New King James Version (NKJV) Copyright © 1982 by Thomas Nelson, Inc. Used by permission.

The New American Standard Bible®, (NASB) Copyright © 1960, 1962, 1963, 1968, 1971, 1972, 1973, 1975, 1977, 1995 by The Lockman Foundation. Used by permission.

The Holman Christian Standard Bible™ (HCSB) Copyright © 1999, 2000, 2001 by Holman Bible Publishers. Used by permission.

Cover Design by Scott Williams/ Richmond & Williams
Page Layout by Bart Dawson

ISBN 978-1-60587-379-4

1 2 3 4 5—RRD—16 15 14 13 12

Printed in China

Presented to

Lily

Gifted by

Mom

On the Date of

December 25, 201

I said a prayer for
you today

my daughter

Introduction

Because you're reading this book, you're probably the fortunate daughter of a loving, praying parent. If so, congratulations. You can be sure that God hears every prayer made on your behalf.

This book is intended to remind you of the love, the concern, the care, the prayers, and the principles that Christian parents (like yours) offer to their children. So, during the next 30 days, please try this experiment: read a chapter each day. If you're already committed to a daily worship time, this book will enrich that experience—if not, the simple act of giving God a few minutes each morning will change the direction of your day and the quality of your life.

As you contemplate your own circumstances, remember this: whatever the size of your challenges, God is bigger. Much bigger. He will instruct you, protect you, energize you, and heal you if you let Him. So pray fervently, listen carefully, work diligently, and hope mightily. When you do so, you and your loved ones can expect the best, not only for the day ahead, but also for all eternity.

My Special Prayer

for you today...

Be confident
every day because
you are in the
hands of God. I
will unfortanately
let you down from
time to time
because I am human.
God will not! You are
an amazing, talented,
smart child of God. Be
strong and pray every day.

Amen

I said a prayer for you today . . .
I prayed that your heart
will be touched
by God's Word.

Heaven and earth will pass away,
but My words will never pass away.

—

Matthew 24:35 HCSB

THE POWER OF HIS PROMISES

God's promises are found in a book like no other: the Holy Bible. The Bible is a road map for life here on earth and for life eternal. As Christians, we are called upon to trust its promises, to follow its commandments, and to share its Good News.

As believers, we must study the Bible each day and meditate upon its meaning for our lives. Otherwise, we deprive ourselves of a priceless gift from our Creator. God's Holy Word is, indeed, a transforming, life-changing, one-of-a-kind treasure. And, a passing acquaintance with the Good Book is insufficient for Christians who seek to obey God's Word and to understand His will.

> The Scriptures were not given for our information, but for our transformation.
>
> —
>
> D. L. Moody

God has made promises to mankind and to you. God's promises never fail and they never grow old. You must trust those promises and share them with your family, with your friends, and with the world.

MORE FROM GOD'S WORD

But the word of the Lord endures forever. And this is the word that was preached as the gospel to you.

1 Peter 1:25 HCSB

All Scripture is inspired by God and is profitable for teaching, for rebuking, for correcting, for training in righteousness, so that the man of God may be complete, equipped for every good work.

2 Timothy 3:16-17 HCSB

For the word of God is living and effective and sharper than any two-edged sword, penetrating as far as to divide soul, spirit, joints, and marrow; it is a judge of the ideas and thoughts of the heart.

Hebrews 4:12 HCSB

The one who is from God listens to God's words. This is why you don't listen, because you are not from God.

John 8:47 HCSB

MORE GREAT IDEAS

Words fail to express my love for this holy Book, my gratitude for its author, for His love and goodness. How shall I thank Him for it?

Lottie Moon

Weave the unveiling fabric of God's word through your heart and mind. It will hold strong, even if the rest of life unravels.

Gigi Graham Tchividjian

I need the spiritual revival that comes from spending quiet time alone with Jesus in prayer and in thoughtful meditation on His Word.

Anne Graham Lotz

God's Word is a light not only to our path but also to our thinking. Place it in your heart today, and you will never walk in darkness.

Joni Eareckson Tada

God can see clearly no matter how dark or foggy the night is. Trust His Word to guide you safely home.

Lisa Whelchel

Walking in faith brings you to the Word of God. There you will be healed, cleansed, fed, nurtured, equipped, and matured.

Kay Arthur

If we are not continually fed with God's Word, we will starve spiritually.

Stormie Omartian

A TIMELY TIP

Charles Swindoll writes, "There are four words I wish we would never forget, and they are, 'God keeps his word.'" And, when it comes to studying God's Word, school is always in session.

Chapter 2

I said a prayer for you today . . .
I prayed that you will
experience God's peace today,
tomorrow, and forever.

Peace I leave with you, My peace I give to you;
not as the world gives do I give to you.
Let not your heart be troubled,
neither let it be afraid.

—

John 14:27 NKJV

PEACE FOR THE JOURNEY

The beautiful words of John 14:27 give us hope: "Peace I leave with you, my peace I give unto you . . ." Jesus offers us peace, not as the world gives, but as He alone gives. We, as believers, can accept His peace or ignore it.

When we accept the peace of Jesus Christ into our hearts, our lives are transformed. And then, because we possess the gift of peace, we can share that gift with fellow Christians, family members, friends, and associates. If, on the other hand, we choose to ignore the gift of peace—for whatever reason—we cannot share what we do not possess.

Peace can be a scarce commodity in a demanding, modern world. How, then, can we find the peace that we so desperately desire? By turning our days and our lives over to God. Elisabeth Elliot writes, "If my life is surrendered to God, all is well. Let me not grab it back, as though it were in peril in His hand but would be safer in mine!" May we give our lives, our hopes, and our prayers to the Lord, and, by doing so, accept His will and His peace.

MORE FROM GOD'S WORD

God has called us to peace.

1 Corinthians 7:15 NKJV

Be of good comfort, be of one mind, live in peace; and the God of love and peace will be with you.

2 Corinthians 13:11 NKJV

For He is our peace.

Ephesians 2:14 HCSB

The result of righteousness will be peace; the effect of righteousness will be quiet confidence forever.

Isaiah 32:17 HCSB

Now the fruit of righteousness is sown in peace by those who make peace.

James 3:18 NKJV

MORE GREAT IDEAS

When we do what is right, we have content-ment, peace, and happiness.

Beverly LaHaye

To know God as He really is—in His essential nature and character—is to arrive at a citadel of peace that circumstances may storm, but can never capture.

Catherine Marshall

I believe that in every time and place it is within our power to acquiesce in the will of God—and what peace it brings to do so!

Elisabeth Elliot

God is in control of history; it's His story. Doesn't that give you a great peace—especially when world events seems so tumultuous and insane?

Kay Arthur

Peace does not mean to be in a place where there is no noise, trouble, or hard work. Peace means to be in the midst of all those things and still be calm in your heart.

Catherine Marshall

The fruit of our placing all things in God's hands is the presence of His abiding peace in our hearts.

Hannah Whitall Smith

In the center of a hurricane there is absolute quiet and peace. There is no safer place than in the center of the will of God.

Corrie ten Boom

A TIMELY TIP

Do you want to discover God's peace? Then do your best to live in the center of God's will.

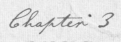

Chapter 3

I said a prayer for you today . . .
I prayed that you will
experience God's perfect joy.

These things I have spoken to you,
that My joy may remain in you,
and that your joy may be full.

—

John 15:11 NKJV

A JOYFUL SPIRIT

God's Word makes it clear: He intends that His joy should become our joy. The Lord intends that believers should share His love with His joy in their hearts. Yet sometimes, amid the inevitable hustle and bustle of life here on earth, we can forfeit—albeit temporarily—God's joy as we wrestle with the challenges of daily living.

Joni Eareckson Tada spoke for Christian women of every generation when she observed, "I wanted the deepest part of me to vibrate with that ancient yet familiar longing, that desire for something that would fill and overflow my soul."

When your heart is heavy, turn to Christ. He will give you peace and joy. And if you already have the joy of Christ in your heart, share it freely, just as Christ has freely shared His joy with you.

MORE FROM GOD'S WORD

Weeping may spend the night, but there is joy in the morning.

Psalm 30:5 HCSB

Rejoice in the Lord always. I will say it again: Rejoice!

Philippians 4:4 HCSB

Make me to hear joy and gladness.

Psalm 51:8 KJV

Now I am coming to You, and I speak these things in the world so that they may have My joy completed in them.

John 17:13 HCSB

A joyful heart makes a face cheerful.

Proverbs 15:13 HCSB

MORE GREAT IDEAS

If you're a thinking Christian, you will be a joyful Christian.

Marie T. Freeman

There may be no trumpet sound or loud applause when we make a right decision, just a calm sense of resolution and peace.

Gloria Gaither

The Christian lifestyle is not one of legalistic do's and don'ts, but one that is positive, attractive, and joyful.

Vonette Bright

To a world that was spiritually dry and populated with parched lives scorched by sin, Jesus was the Living Water who would quench the thirsty soul, saving it from "bondage" and filling it with satisfaction and joy and purpose and meaning.

Anne Graham Lotz

Jesus did not promise to change the circumstances around us. He promised great peace and pure joy to those who would learn to believe that God actually controls all things.

Corrie ten Boom

What is your focus today? Joy comes when it is Jesus first, others second . . . then you.

Kay Arthur

Joy is a by-product not of happy circumstances, education or talent, but of a healthy relationship with God and a determination to love Him no matter what.

Barbara Johnson

A TIMELY TIP

Joy does not depend upon your circumstances but upon your relationship with God.

Chapter 4

I said a prayer for you today . . .
I prayed that you will
receive God's perfect love.

For the Lord is good, and His love is eternal;
His faithfulness endures through all generations.

—

Psalm 100:5 HCSB

EMBRACED BY GOD

God's love for you is bigger and better than you can imagine. In fact, God's love is far too big to comprehend (in this lifetime). But this much we know: God loves you so much that He sent His Son Jesus to come to this earth and to die for you. And, when you accepted Jesus into your heart, God gave you a gift that is more precious than gold: the gift of eternal life.

The words of Romans 8 make this promise: "For I am persuaded that neither death nor life, nor angels nor principalities nor powers, nor things present nor things to come, nor height nor depth, nor any other created thing, shall be able to separate us from the love of God which is in Christ Jesus our Lord" (vv. 38-39 NKJV).

Sometimes, in the crush of your daily duties, God may seem far away, but He is not. God is everywhere you have ever been and everywhere you will ever go. He is with you night and day; He knows your thoughts and He hears your prayers. When you earnestly seek Him, you will find Him because He is here, waiting patiently for you to reach out to Him.

MORE FROM GOD'S WORD

For God so loved the world, that he gave his only begotten Son, that whosoever believeth in him should not perish, but have everlasting life.

John 3:16 KJV

[Because of] the Lord's faithful love we do not perish, for His mercies never end. They are new every morning; great is Your faithfulness!

Lamentations 3:22-23 HCSB

Help me, Lord my God; save me according to Your faithful love.

Psalm 109:26 HCSB

Whoever is wise will observe these things, and they will understand the lovingkindness of the Lord.

Psalm 107:43 NKJV

A person's insight gives him patience, and his virtue is to overlook an offense.

Proverbs 19:11 HCSB

MORE GREAT IDEAS

God is a God of unconditional, unremitting love, a love that corrects and chastens but never ceases.

Kay Arthur

There is no pit so deep that God's love is not deeper still.

Corrie ten Boom

Jesus loves us with fidelity, purity, constancy, and passion, no matter how imperfect we are.

Stormie Omartian

The fact is, God no longer deals with us in judgment but in mercy. If people got what they deserved, this old planet would have ripped apart at the seams centuries ago. Praise God that because of His great love "we are not consumed, for his compassions never fail" (Lam. 3:22).

Joni Eareckson Tada

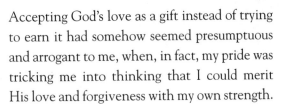

Accepting God's love as a gift instead of trying to earn it had somehow seemed presumptuous and arrogant to me, when, in fact, my pride was tricking me into thinking that I could merit His love and forgiveness with my own strength.

Lisa Whelchel

Snuggle in God's arms. When you are hurting, when you feel lonely or left out, let Him cradle you, comfort you, reassure you of His all-sufficient power and love.

Kay Arthur

Being loved by Him whose opinion matters most gives us the security to risk loving, too—even loving ourselves.

Gloria Gaither

A TIMELY TIP

Remember: God's love for you is too big to understand with your brain . . . but it's not too big to feel with your heart.

Chapter 5

I said a prayer for you today . . .
I prayed that you will
discover God's purpose
for your life.

*For it is God who is working among you
both the willing and the working
for His good purpose.*

—

Philippians 2:13 HCSB

FINDING PURPOSE

Life is best lived on purpose. And purpose, like everything else in the universe, begins with God. Whether you realize it or not, God has a plan for your life, a divine calling, a direction in which He is leading you. When you welcome God into your heart and establish a genuine relationship with Him, He will begin, in time, to make His purposes known.

Sometimes, God's intentions will be clear to you; other times, God's plan will seem uncertain at best. But even on those difficult days when you are unsure which way to turn, you must never lose sight of these overriding facts: God created you for a reason; He has important work for you to do; and He's waiting patiently for you to do it.

And the next step is up to you.

> His life is our light—our purpose and meaning and reason for living.
>
> —
>
> Anne Graham Lotz

MORE FROM GOD'S WORD

We know that all things work together for the good of those who love God: those who are called according to His purpose.

Romans 8:28 HCSB

I will instruct you and show you the way to go; with My eye on you, I will give counsel.

Psalm 32:8 HCSB

You reveal the path of life to me; in Your presence is abundant joy; in Your right hand are eternal pleasures.

Psalm 16:11 HCSB

Commit your activities to the Lord and your plans will be achieved.

Proverbs 16:3 HCSB

To everything there is a season, a time for every purpose under heaven.

Ecclesiastes 3:1 NKJV

MORE GREAT IDEAS

Only God's chosen task for you will ultimately satisfy. Do not wait until it is too late to realize the privilege of serving Him in His chosen position for you.

Beth Moore

In the very place where God has put us, whatever its limitations, whatever kind of work it may be, we may indeed serve the Lord Christ.

Elisabeth Elliot

How much of our lives are, well, so daily. How often our hours are filled with the mundane, seemingly unimportant things that have to be done, whether at home or work. These very "daily" tasks could become a celebration of praise. "It is through consecration," someone has said, "that drudgery is made divine."

Gigi Graham Tchividjian

Yesterday is just experience but tomorrow is glistening with purpose—and today is the channel leading from one to the other.

Barbara Johnson

If you want purpose and meaning and satisfaction and fulfillment and peace and hope and joy and abundant life that lasts forever, look to Jesus.

Anne Graham Lotz

God specializes in things fresh and firsthand. His plans for you this year may outshine those of the past. He's prepared to fill your days with reasons to give Him praise.

Joni Eareckson Tada

A TIMELY TIP

God has a wonderful plan for your life. And the time to start looking for that plan—and living it—is now.

Chapter 6

I said a prayer for you today . . .
I prayed that you will focus
your thoughts on God's infinite
blessings, not on life's
inevitable hardships.

*Finally brothers, whatever is true, whatever is
honorable, whatever is just, whatever is pure,
whatever is lovely, whatever is commendable—
if there is any moral excellence and if there is
any praise—dwell on these things.*

—

Philippians 4:8 HCSB

OPTIMISM NOW

Pessimism and Christianity don't mix. Why? Because Christians have every reason to be optimistic about life here on earth and life eternal. Mrs. Charles E. Cowman advised, "Never yield to gloomy anticipation. Place your hope and confidence in God. He has no record of failure."

Sometimes, despite our trust in God, we may fall into the spiritual traps of worry, frustration, anxiety, or sheer exhaustion, and our hearts become heavy. What's needed is plenty of rest, a large dose of perspective, and God's healing touch, but not necessarily in that order.

Today, make this promise to yourself and keep it: vow to be a hope-filled Christian. Think optimistically about your life, your profession, and your future. Trust your hopes, not your fears. Take time to celebrate God's glorious creation. And then, when you've filled your heart with hope and gladness, share your optimism with others. They'll be better for it, and so will you. But not necessarily in that order.

MORE FROM GOD'S WORD

Make me hear joy and gladness.

Psalm 51:8 NKJV

My cup runs over. Surely goodness and mercy shall follow me all the days of my life; and I will dwell in the house of the Lord Forever.

Psalm 23:5-6 NKJV

But if we hope for what we do not see, we eagerly wait for it with patience.

Romans 8:25 HCSB

For God has not given us a spirit of fearfulness, but one of power, love, and sound judgment.

2 Timothy 1:7 HCSB

Be strong and courageous, all you who put your hope in the LORD.

Psalm 31:24 HCSB

MORE GREAT IDEAS

The Christian lifestyle is not one of legalistic do's and don'ts, but one that is positive, attractive, and joyful.

Vonette Bright

It never hurts your eyesight to look on the bright side of things.

Barbara Johnson

Make the least of all that goes and the most of all that comes. Don't regret what is past. Cherish what you have. Look forward to all that is to come. And most important of all, rely moment by moment on Jesus Christ.

Gigi Graham Tchividjian

We may run, walk, stumble, drive, or fly, but let us never lose sight of the reason for the journey, or miss a chance to see a rainbow on the way.

Gloria Gaither

Never yield to gloomy anticipation. Place your hope and confidence in God. He has no record of failure.

Mrs. Charles E. Cowman

If you can't tell whether your glass is half-empty or half-full, you don't need another glass; what you need is better eyesight . . . and a more thankful heart.

Marie T. Freeman

Don't miss the beautiful colors of the rainbow while you're looking for the pot of gold at the end of it!

Barbara Johnson

A TIMELY TIP

Be positive: If your thoughts tend toward the negative end of the spectrum, redirect them. How? You can start by counting your blessings and by thanking your Father in heaven.

Chapter 7

I said a prayer for you today . . .
I prayed that you will always know how much you are loved.

Now these three remain: faith, hope, and love.
But the greatest of these is love.
—

1 Corinthians 13:13 HCSB

YOU ARE LOVED

Make no mistake: you are loved. Your family loves you, your closest friends love you, and God loves you. How will you respond to their love? Jesus clearly defined what your response should be: "'Love the Lord your God with all your heart and with all your soul and with all your mind.' This is the first and greatest commandment. And the second is like it: 'Love your neighbor as yourself.' All the Law and the Prophets hang on these two commandments" (Matthew 22:37-40 NIV).

Today, as you meet the demands of everyday living, will you pause long enough to return God's love? And then will you share it? Prayerfully, you will. When you embrace God's love, you are forever changed. When you embrace God's love, you feel differently about yourself, your family, your friends, and your world. When you embrace God's love, you have enough love to keep and enough love to share: enough love for a day, enough love for a lifetime, enough love for all eternity.

MORE FROM GOD'S WORD

I pray that you, being rooted and firmly established in love, may be able to comprehend with all the saints what is the breadth and width, height and depth, and to know the Messiah's love that surpasses knowledge, so you may be filled with all the fullness of God.

Ephesians 3:17-19 HCSB

If I speak the languages of men and of angels, but do not have love, I am a sounding gong or a clanging cymbal.

1 Corinthians 13:1 HCSB

Dear friends, if God loved us in this way, we also must love one another.

1 John 4:11 HCSB

We love because He first loved us.

1 John 4:19 HCSB

MORE GREAT IDEAS

Love is not soft as water is; it is solid as a rock on which the waves of hatred beat in vain.

Corrie ten Boom

Love always means sacrifice.

Elisabeth Elliot

Line by line, moment by moment, special times are etched into our memories in the permanent ink of everlasting love in our relationships.

Gloria Gaither

Love is extravagant in the price it is willing to pay, the time it is willing to give, the hardships it is willing to endure, and the strength it is willing to spend. Love never thinks in terms of "how little," but always in terms of "how much." Love gives, love knows, and love lasts.

Joni Eareckson Tada

Love is the seed of all hope. It is the enticement to trust, to risk, to try, and to go on.

Gloria Gaither

Prayer is the ultimate love language. It communicates in ways we can't.

Stormie Omartian

Agape is a kind of love God demonstrates to one person through another.

Beth Moore

Forgiveness is the precondition of love.

Catherine Marshall

A TIMELY TIP

God is love, and He expects us to share His love.

Chapter 8

I said a prayer for you today . . .
I prayed that you will
experience God's presence today
and every day of your life.

*Draw near to God,
and He will draw near to you.*

—

James 4:8 HCSB

SENSING GOD'S PRESENCE

Since God is everywhere, we are free to sense His presence whenever we take the time to quiet our souls and turn our prayers to Him. But sometimes, amid the incessant demands of everyday life, we turn our thoughts far from God; when we do, we suffer.

Do you set aside quiet moments each day to offer praise to your Creator? As a woman who has received the gift of God's grace, you most certainly should. Silence is a gift that you give to yourself and to God. During these moments of stillness, you will often sense the infinite love and power of your Creator—and He, in turn, will speak directly to your heart.

The familiar words of Psalm 46:10 remind us to "be still, and know that I am God." When we do so, we encounter the awesome presence of our loving Heavenly Father, and we are comforted in the knowledge that God is not just near. He is here.

> God wants to be in our leisure time as much as He is in our churches and in our work.
>
> —
>
> Beth Moore

MORE FROM GOD'S WORD

You will seek Me and find Me when you search for Me with all your heart.

Jeremiah 29:13 HCSB

The Lord is near all who call out to Him, all who call out to Him with integrity. He fulfills the desires of those who fear Him; He hears their cry for help and saves them.

Psalm 145:18-19 HCSB

Surely goodness and mercy shall follow me all the days of my life: and I will dwell in the house of the Lord for ever.

Psalm 23:6 KJV

I am not alone, because the Father is with Me.

John 16:32 HCSB

I have set the Lord always before me; because He is at my right hand I shall not be moved.

Psalm 16:8 NKJV

MORE GREAT IDEAS

If you want to hear God's voice clearly and you are uncertain, then remain in His presence until He changes that uncertainty. Often, much can happen during this waiting for the Lord. Sometimes, He changes pride into humility, doubt into faith and peace.

Corrie ten Boom

Give yourself a gift today: be present with yourself. God is. Enjoy your own personality. God does.

Barbara Johnson

If your heart has grown cold, it is because you have moved away from the fire of His presence.

Beth Moore

It is God to whom and with whom we travel, and while He is the End of our journey, He is also at every stopping place.

Elisabeth Elliot

Through the death and broken body of Jesus Christ on the Cross, you and I have been given access to the presence of God when we approach Him by faith in prayer.

Anne Graham Lotz

Our souls were made to live in an upper atmosphere, and we stifle and choke if we live on any lower level. Our eyes were made to look off from these heavenly heights, and our vision is distorted by any lower gazing.

Hannah Whitall Smith

Oh! what a Savior, gracious to all, / Oh! how His blessings round us fall, / Gently to comfort, kindly to cheer, / Sleeping or waking, God is near.

Fanny Crosby

A TIMELY TIP

If you're here, God is here. If you're there, God is, too. You can't get away from Him or His love . . . thank goodness!

I said a prayer for you today . . .
I prayed that you will be
quick to forgive everyone,
including yourself.

And whenever you stand praying,
if you have anything against anyone,
forgive him, so that your Father in heaven
may also forgive you your wrongdoing.

—

Mark 11:25 HCSB

FORGIVENESS NOW

Forgiveness is seldom easy, but it is always right. When we forgive those who have hurt us, we honor God by obeying His commandments. But when we harbor bitterness against others, we disobey God—with predictably unhappy results.

> To be a Christian means to forgive the inexcusable, because God has forgiven the inexcusable in you.
>
> —
>
> C. S. Lewis

Are you easily frustrated by the inevitable shortcomings of others? If so, perhaps you need a refresher course in the art of forgiveness.

If there exists even one person, alive or dead, whom you have not forgiven (and that includes yourself), follow God's commandment and His will for your life: forgive that person today. And remember that bitterness, anger, and regret are not part of God's plan for your life. Forgiveness is.

MORE FROM GOD'S WORD

Be merciful, just as your Father also is merciful.

Luke 6:36 HCSB

All bitterness, anger and wrath, insult and slander must be removed from you, along with all wickedness. And be kind and compassionate to one another, forgiving one another, just as God also forgave you in Christ.

Ephesians 4:31-32 HCSB

Then Peter came to Him and said, "Lord, how many times could my brother sin against me and I forgive him? As many as seven times?" "I tell you, not as many as seven," Jesus said to him, "but 70 times seven."

Matthew 18:21-22 HCSB

A person's insight gives him patience, and his virtue is to overlook an offense.

Proverbs 19:11 HCSB

MORE GREAT IDEAS

How often should you forgive the other person? Only as many times as you want God to forgive you!

Marie T. Freeman

Forgiveness is actually the best revenge because it not only sets us free from the person we forgive, but it frees us to move into all that God has in store for us.

Stormie Omartian

God expects us to forgive others as He has forgiven us; we are to follow His example by having a forgiving heart.

Vonette Bright

Forgiveness is the key that unlocks the door of resentment and the handcuffs of hate. It is a power that breaks the chains of bitterness and the shackles of selfishness.

Corrie ten Boom

I believe that forgiveness can become a continuing cycle: because God forgives us, we're to forgive others; because we forgive others, God forgives us. Scripture presents both parts of the cycle.

Shirley Dobson

Sometimes, we need a housecleaning of the heart.

Catherine Marshall

Forgiveness is contagious. First you forgive them, and pretty soon, they'll forgive you, too.

Marie T. Freeman

A TIMELY TIP

Today, make a list of the people you still need to forgive. Then make up your mind to forgive at least one person on that list. Finally, ask God to cleanse your heart of bitterness, animosity, and regret. If you ask Him sincerely and often, He will respond.

I said a prayer for you today . . .
I prayed that you will
always trust God.

Trust in the Lord with all your heart,
and do not rely on your own understanding;
think about Him in all your ways,
and He will guide you on the right paths.

—

Proverbs 3:5-6 HCSB

TRUST HIM

When our dreams come true and our plans prove successful, we find it easy to thank our Creator and easy to trust His divine providence. But in times of sorrow or hardship, we may find ourselves questioning God's plans for our lives.

On occasion, you will confront circumstances that trouble you to the very core of your soul. It is during these difficult days that you must find the wisdom and the courage to trust your Heavenly Father despite your circumstances.

Do you seek God's blessings? Then trust Him. Trust Him with your relationships. Trust Him with your priorities. Follow His commandments and pray for His guidance. Trust Your Heavenly Father day by day, moment by moment—in good times and in trying times. Then, wait patiently for God's revelations . . . and prepare yourself for the abundance and peace that will most certainly be yours when you do.

MORE FROM GOD'S WORD

For the eyes of the Lord range throughout the earth to show Himself strong for those whose hearts are completely His.

2 Chronicles 16:9 HCSB

He granted their request because they trusted in Him.

1 Chronicles 5:20 HCSB

Let us hold fast the confession of our hope without wavering, for He who promised is faithful.

Hebrews 10:23 NKJV

The one who understands a matter finds success, and the one who trusts in the Lord will be happy.

Proverbs 16:20 HCSB

I know whom I have believed and am persuaded that He is able to guard what has been entrusted to me until that day.

2 Timothy 1:12 HCSB

MORE GREAT IDEAS

Sometimes the very essence of faith is trusting God in the midst of things He knows good and well we cannot comprehend.

Beth Moore

Are you serious about wanting God's guidance to become the person he wants you to be? The first step is to tell God that you know you can't manage your own life; that you need his help.

Catherine Marshall

Brother, is your faith looking upward today? / Trust in the promise of the Savior. / Sister, is the light shining bright on your way? / Trust in the promise of thy Lord.

Fanny Crosby

Never be afraid to trust an unknown future to a known God.

Corrie ten Boom

As God's children, we are the recipients of lavish love—a love that motivates us to keep trusting even when we have no idea what God is doing.

Beth Moore

Once we recognize our need for Jesus, then the building of our faith begins. It is a daily, moment-by-moment life of absolute dependence upon Him for everything.

Catherine Marshall

When the train goes through a tunnel and the world becomes dark, do you jump out? Of course not. You sit still and trust the engineer to get you through.

Corrie ten Boom

A TIMELY TIP

One of the most important lessons that you can ever learn is to trust God for everything—not some things, not most things . . . everything!

Chapter 11

I said a prayer for you today . . .
I prayed that you will
understand the power
of patience.

Rejoice in hope; be patient in affliction;
be persistent in prayer.

—

Romans 12:12 HCSB

THE POWER OF PATIENCE

Most of us are impatient for God to grant us the desires of our heart. Usually, we know what we want, and we know precisely when we want it: right now, if not sooner. But God may have other plans. And when God's plans differ from our own, we must trust in His infinite wisdom and in His infinite love.

> Waiting is an essential part of spiritual discipline. It can be the ultimate test of faith.
>
> —
>
> Anne Graham Lotz

As busy people living in a fast-paced world, many of us find that waiting quietly for God is difficult. Why? Because we are fallible human beings seeking to live according to our own timetables, not God's. In our better moments, we realize that patience is not only a virtue, but it is also a commandment from God.

God instructs us to be patient in all things. We must be patient with our families, our friends, and our associates. We must also be patient with our Creator as He unfolds His plan for our lives.

MORE FROM GOD'S WORD

Love is patient; love is kind.

1 Corinthians 13:4 HCSB

A patient spirit is better than a proud spirit.

Ecclesiastes 7:8 HCSB

Therefore the Lord is waiting to show you mercy, and is rising up to show you compassion, for the Lord is a just God. Happy are all who wait patiently for Him.

Isaiah 30:18 HCSB

Be gentle to everyone, able to teach, and patient.

2 Timothy 2:23 HCSB

My brethren, count it all joy when you fall into various trials, knowing that the testing of your faith produces patience. But let patience have its perfect work, that you may be perfect and complete, lacking nothing.

James 1:2-4 NKJV

MORE GREAT IDEAS

We must learn to wait. There is grace supplied to the one who waits.

Mrs. Charles E. Cowman

How do you wait upon the Lord? First you must learn to sit at His feet and take time to listen to His words.

Kay Arthur

Waiting is the hardest kind of work, but God knows best, and we may joyfully leave all in His hands.

Lottie Moon

If you want to hear God's voice clearly and you are uncertain, then remain in His presence until He changes that uncertainty. Often much can happen during this waiting for the Lord. Sometimes He changes pride into humility; doubt into faith and peace.

Corrie ten Boom

Let me encourage you to continue to wait with faith. God may not perform a miracle, but He is trustworthy to touch you and make you whole where there used to be a hole.

Lisa Whelchel

When we read of the great Biblical leaders, we see that it was not uncommon for God to ask them to wait, not just a day or two, but for years, until God was ready for them to act.

Gloria Gaither

Those who have had to wait and work for happiness seem to enjoy it more, because they never take it for granted.

Barbara Johnson

A TIMELY TIP

When you learn to be more patient with others, you'll make your world—and your heart—a better place.

Chapter 12

I said a prayer for you today . . .
I prayed that your faith
will be strong.

*For whatever is born of God
overcomes the world. And this is the victory
that has overcome the world—our faith.*

—

1 John 5:4 NKJV

FAITH IN THE FATHER

A suffering woman sought healing in an unusual way: she simply touched the hem of Jesus' garment. When she did, Jesus turned and said, "Daughter, be of good comfort; thy faith hath made thee whole" (Matthew 9:22 KJV). We, too, can be made whole when we place our faith completely and unwaveringly in the person of Jesus Christ.

When you place your faith, your trust, indeed your life in the hands of Christ Jesus, you'll be amazed at the marvelous things He can do with you and through you. So strengthen your faith through praise, through worship, through Bible study, and through prayer. Then, trust God's plans. Your Heavenly Father is standing at the door of your heart. If you reach out to Him in faith, He will give you peace and heal your broken spirit. Be content to touch even the smallest fragment of the Master's garment, and He will make you whole.

> If God chooses to remain silent, faith is content.
>
> —
>
> Ruth Bell Graham

MORE FROM GOD'S WORD

Now faith is the reality of what is hoped for, the proof of what is not seen.

Hebrews 11:1 HCSB

Now without faith it is impossible to please God, for the one who draws near to Him must believe that He exists and rewards those who seek Him.

Hebrews 11:6 HCSB

For we walk by faith, not by sight.

2 Corinthians 5:7 HCSB

If you do not stand firm in your faith, then you will not stand at all.

Isaiah 7:9 HCSB

Indeed, God is my salvation. I will trust [Him] and not be afraid. Because Yah, the LORD, is my strength and my song, He has become my salvation.

Isaiah 12:2 HCSB

MORE GREAT IDEAS

Just as our faith strengthens our prayer life, so do our prayers deepen our faith. Let us pray often, starting today, for a deeper, more powerful faith.

Shirley Dobson

Faith is nothing more or less than actively trusting God.

Catherine Marshall

Faith does not concern itself with the entire journey. One step is enough.

Mrs. Charles E. Cowman

When you and I place our faith in Jesus Christ and invite Him to come live within us, the Holy Spirit comes upon us, and the power of God overshadows us, and the life of Jesus is born within us.

Anne Graham Lotz

Sometimes the very essence of faith is trusting God in the midst of things He knows good and well we cannot comprehend.

Beth Moore

Faith is seeing light with the eyes of your heart, when the eyes of your body see only darkness.

Barbara Johnson

Grace calls you to get up, throw off your blanket of helplessness, and to move on through life in faith.

Kay Arthur

A TIMELY TIP

The quality of your faith will help determine the quality of your day and the quality of your life.

Chapter 13

I said a prayer for you today . . .
I prayed that you will find
strength in God.

And He said to me,
"My grace is sufficient for you,
for My strength is made perfect in weakness."

—

2 Corinthians 12:9 NKJV

STRENGTH FOR THE JOURNEY

Where do you go to find strength? The gym? The health food store? The espresso bar? There's a better source of strength, of course, and that source is God. He is a never-ending source of strength and courage if you call upon Him.

Are you an energized Christian? You should be. But if you're not, you must seek strength and renewal from the source that will never fail: that source, of course, is your Heavenly Father. And rest assured—when you sincerely petition Him, He will give you all the strength you need to live victoriously for Him.

Have you "tapped in" to the power of God? Have you turned your life and your heart over to Him, or are you muddling along under your own power? The answer to this question will determine the quality of your life here on earth and the destiny of your life throughout all eternity. So start tapping in—and remember that when it comes to strength, God is the Ultimate Source.

MORE FROM GOD'S WORD

You, therefore, my child, be strong in the grace that is in Christ Jesus.

2 Timothy 2:1 HCSB

The Lord is my strength and my song; He has become my salvation.

Exodus 15:2 HCSB

He gives strength to the weary and strengthens the powerless.

Isaiah 40:29 HCSB

But those who wait on the Lord shall renew their strength; they shall mount up with wings like eagles, they shall run and not be weary, they shall walk and not faint.

Isaiah 40:31 NKJV

Finally, be strengthened by the Lord and by His vast strength.

Ephesians 6:10 HCSB

MORE GREAT IDEAS

Worry does not empty tomorrow of its sorrow; it empties today of its strength.

Corrie ten Boom

One reason so much American Christianity is a mile wide and an inch deep is that Christians are simply tired. Sometimes you need to kick back and rest for Jesus' sake.

Dennis Swanberg

God does not dispense strength and encouragement like a druggist fills your prescription. The Lord doesn't promise to give us something to take so we can handle our weary moments. He promises us Himself. That is all. And that is enough.

Charles Swindoll

We are never stronger than the moment we admit we are weak.

Beth Moore

When the dream of our heart is one that God has planted there, a strange happiness flows into us. At that moment, all of the spiritual resources of the universe are released to help us. Our praying is then at one with the will of God and becomes a channel for the Creator's purposes for us and our world.

Catherine Marshall

When you and I are related to Jesus Christ, our strength and wisdom and peace and joy and love and hope may run out, but His life rushes in to keep us filled to the brim. We are showered with blessings, not because of anything we have or have not done, but simply because of Him.

Anne Graham Lotz

A TIMELY TIP

When you are tired, fearful, or discouraged, God can restore your strength.

I said a prayer for you today . . .
I prayed that you will
establish God's priorities for
your day and your life.

He said to them all, *"If anyone desires to come
after Me, let him deny himself, and take up his
cross daily, and follow Me. For whoever desires
to save his life will lose it, but whoever loses
his life for My sake will save it."*

—

Luke 9:23-24 NKJV

PRIORITIES FOR THE JOURNEY

"First things first." These words are easy to speak but hard to put into practice. For busy women living in a demanding world, placing first things first can be difficult indeed. Why? Because so many people are expecting so many things from us!

If you're having trouble prioritizing your day, perhaps you've been trying to organize your life according to your own plans, not God's. A better strategy, of course, is to take your daily obligations and place them in the hands of the One who created you. To do so, you must prioritize your day according to God's commandments, and you must seek His will and His wisdom in all matters. Then, you can face the day with the assurance that the same God who created our universe out of nothingness will help you place first things first in your own life.

Do you feel overwhelmed or confused? Turn the concerns of this day over to God—prayerfully, earnestly, and often. Then listen for His answer . . . and trust the answer He gives.

MORE FROM GOD'S WORD

And I pray this: that your love will keep on growing in knowledge and every kind of discernment, so that you can determine what really matters and can be pure and blameless in the day of Christ.

Philippians 1:9 HCSB

Now it happened as they went that He entered a certain village; and a certain woman named Martha welcomed Him into her house. And she had a sister called Mary, who also sat at Jesus' feet and heard His word. But Martha was distracted with much serving, and she approached Him and said, "Lord, do You not care that my sister has left me to serve alone? Therefore tell her to help me." And Jesus answered and said to her, "Martha, Martha, you are worried and troubled about many things. But one thing is needed, and Mary has chosen that good part, which will not be taken away from her."

Luke 10:38-42 NKJV

For where your treasure is, there your heart will be also.

Luke 12:34 HCSB

MORE GREAT IDEAS

Sin is largely a matter of mistaken priorities. Any sin in us that is cherished, hidden, and not confessed will cut the nerve center of our faith.

Catherine Marshall

Have you prayed about your resources lately? Find out how God wants you to use your time and your money. No matter what it costs, forsake all that is not of God.

Kay Arthur

Great relief and satisfaction can come from seeking God's priorities for us in each season, discerning what is "best" in the midst of many noble opportunities, and pouring our most excellent energies into those things.

Beth Moore

The work of God is appointed. There is always enough time to do the will of God.

Elisabeth Elliot

It's sobering to contemplate how much time, effort, sacrifice, compromise, and attention we give to acquiring and increasing our supply of something that is totally insignificant in eternity.

Anne Graham Lotz

We set our eyes on the finish line, forgetting the past, and straining toward the mark of spiritual maturity and fruitfulness.

Vonette Bright

The manifold rewards of a serious, consistent prayer life demonstrate clearly that time with our Lord should be our first priority.

Shirley Dobson

A TIMELY TIP

Setting priorities may mean saying no. You don't have time to do everything, so it's perfectly okay to say no to the things that mean less so that you'll have time for the things that mean more.

Chapter 15

I said a prayer for you today . . .
I prayed that you will
always stay strong and
never lose hope.

*For I know the thoughts that I think toward you,
says the Lord, thoughts of peace and not of evil,
to give you a future and a hope.
Then you will call upon Me and go and
pray to Me, and I will listen to you.*

—

Jeremiah 29:11-12 NKJV

BE HOPEFUL

The hope that the world offers is fleeting and imperfect. The hope that God offers is unchanging, unshakable, and unending. It is no wonder, then, that when we seek security from worldly sources, our hopes are often dashed. Thankfully, God has no such record of failure.

Where will you place your hopes today? Will you entrust your future to man or to God? Will you seek solace exclusively from fallible human beings, or will you place your hopes, first and foremost, in the trusting hands of your Creator? The decision is yours, and you must live with the results of the choice you make.

For thoughtful believers, hope begins with God. Period. So today, as you embark upon the next stage of your life's journey, consider the words of the Psalmist: "You are my hope; O Lord GOD, You are my confidence" (71:5 NASB). Then, place your trust in the One who cannot be shaken.

> Hope is the desire and the ability to move forward.
>
> —
>
> Emilie Barnes

MORE FROM GOD'S WORD

Now may the God of hope fill you with all joy and peace in believing, so that you may overflow with hope by the power of the Holy Spirit.

Romans 15:13 HCSB

But if we hope for what we do not see, we eagerly wait for it with patience.

Romans 8:25 HCSB

Rejoice in hope; be patient in affliction; be persistent in prayer.

Romans 12:12 HCSB

Lord, I turn my hope to You. My God, I trust in You. Do not let me be disgraced; do not let my enemies gloat over me.

Psalm 25:1-2 HCSB

Let us hold on to the confession of our hope without wavering, for He who promised is faithful.

Hebrews 10:23 HCSB

MORE GREAT IDEAS

Never yield to gloomy anticipation. Place your hope and confidence in God. He has no record of failure.

Mrs. Charles E. Cowman

I discovered that sorrow was not to be feared but rather endured with hope and expectancy that God would use it to visit and bless my life.

Jill Briscoe

God's Word never said we were not to grieve our losses. It says we are not to grieve as those who have no hope (1 Thessalonians 4:13). Big Difference.

Beth Moore

No other religion, no other philosophy promises new bodies, hearts, and minds. Only in the Gospel of Christ do hurting people find such incredible hope.

Joni Eareckson Tada

When you accept the fact that sometimes seasons are dry and times are hard and that God is in control of both, you will discover a sense of divine refuge because the hope then is in God and not in yourself.

Charles Swindoll

In those desperate times when we feel like we don't have an ounce of strength, He will gently pick up our heads so that our eyes can behold something—something that will keep His hope alive in us.

Kathy Troccoli

A TIMELY TIP

If you're experiencing tough times, you'll be wise to start spending more time with God. And if you do your part, God will do His part. So never be afraid to hope—or to ask—for a miracle.

Chapter 16

I said a prayer for you today . . .
I prayed that you will always
keep growing both spiritually
and emotionally.

*For this reason also, since the day we heard this,
we haven't stopped praying for you.
We are asking that you may be filled
with the knowledge of His will in all wisdom
and spiritual understanding.*

—

Colossians 1:9 HCSB

CONTINUING TO GROW

When will you be a "fully-grown" Christian? Hopefully never—or at least not until you arrive in heaven! As a believer living here on planet earth, you're never "fully grown"; you always have the potential to keep growing.

In those quiet moments when you open your heart to God, the One who made you keeps remaking you. He gives you direction, perspective, wisdom, and courage. And, the appropriate moment to accept those spiritual gifts is always the present one.

Would you like a time-tested formula for spiritual growth? Here it is: keep studying God's Word, keep obeying His commandments, keep praying (and listening for answers), and seek to live in the center of God's will. When you do, you will never be a "stagnant" believer.

> Grow, dear friends, but grow, I beseech you, in God's way, which is the only true way.
>
> —
>
> Hannah Whitall Smith

MORE FROM GOD'S WORD

But grow in the grace and knowledge of our Lord and Savior Jesus Christ. To Him be the glory both now and to the day of eternity.

2 Peter 3:18 HCSB

I want their hearts to be encouraged and joined together in love, so that they may have all the riches of assured understanding, and have the knowledge of God's mystery—Christ.

Colossians 2:2 HCSB

Therefore, leaving the elementary message about the Messiah, let us go on to maturity.

Hebrews 6:1 HCSB

For You, O God, have tested us; You have refined us as silver is refined. You brought us into the net; You laid affliction on our backs. You have caused men to ride over our heads; we went through fire and through water; but You brought us out to rich fulfillment.

Psalm 66:10–12 NKJV

MORE GREAT IDEAS

We set our eyes on the finish line, forgetting the past, and straining toward the mark of spiritual maturity and fruitfulness.

Vonette Bright

We look at our burdens and heavy loads, and we shrink from them. But, if we lift them and bind them about our hearts, they become wings, and on them we can rise and soar toward God.

Mrs. Charles E. Cowman

If all struggles and sufferings were eliminated, the spirit would no more reach maturity than would the child.

Elisabeth Elliot

Growth in depth and strength and consistency and fruitfulness and ultimately in Christlikeness is only possible when the winds of life are contrary to personal comfort.

Anne Graham Lotz

You are either becoming more like Christ every day or you're becoming less like Him. There is no neutral position in the Lord.

Stormie Omartian

God is teaching me to become more and more "teachable": To keep evolving. To keep taking the risk of learning something new . . . or unlearning something old and off base.

Beth Moore

He makes us wait. He keeps us in the dark on purpose. He makes us walk when we want to run, sit still when we want to walk, for he has things to do in our souls that we are not interested in.

Elisabeth Elliot

A TIMELY TIP

Spiritual maturity is a journey, not a destination. A growing relationship with God should be your highest priority.

Chapter 17

I said a prayer for you today . . .
I prayed that you will
find time to be still with God.

Be still, and know that I am God.

—

Psalm 46:10 KJV

BE STILL MY SOUL

We live in a noisy world, a world filled with distractions, frustrations, and complications. But if we allow the distractions of a clamorous world to separate us from God's peace, we do ourselves a profound disservice. If we are to maintain righteous minds and compassionate hearts, we must take time each day for prayer and for meditation. We must make ourselves still in the presence of our Creator. We must quiet our minds and our hearts so that we might sense God's will, God's love, and God's Son.

Has the busy pace of life robbed you of the peace that might otherwise be yours through Jesus Christ? Nothing is more important than the time you spend with your Savior. So be still and claim the inner peace that is your spiritual birthright: the peace of Jesus Christ. It is offered freely; it has been paid for in full; it is yours for the asking. So ask. And then share.

> The world is full of noise. Might we not set ourselves to learn silence, stillness, solitude?
>
> —
>
> Elisabeth Elliot

MORE FROM GOD'S WORD

Be silent before Me.

Isaiah 41:1 HCSB

Be silent before the Lord and wait expectantly for Him.

Psalm 37:7 HCSB

Truly my soul silently waits for God; from Him comes my salvation.

Psalm 62:1 NKJV

My soul, wait silently for God alone, for my expectation is from Him.

Psalm 62:5 NKJV

But those who wait on the Lord shall renew their strength; they shall mount up with wings like eagles, they shall run and not be weary, they shall walk and not faint.

Isaiah 40:31 NKJV

MORE GREAT IDEAS

When we are in the presence of God, removed from distractions, we are able to hear him more clearly, and a secure environment has been established for the young and broken places in our hearts to surface.

John Eldredge

Be quiet enough to hear God's whisper.

Anonymous

Because Jesus Christ is our Great High Priest, not only can we approach God without a human "go-between," we can also hear and learn from God in some sacred moments without one.

Beth Moore

I need the spiritual revival that comes from spending quiet time alone with Jesus in prayer and in thoughtful meditation on His Word.

Anne Graham Lotz

Let your loneliness be transformed into a holy aloneness. Sit still before the Lord. Remember Naomi's word to Ruth: "Sit still, my daughter, until you see how the matter will fall."

Elisabeth Elliot

Instead of waiting for the feeling, wait upon God. You can do this by growing still and quiet, then expressing in prayer what your mind knows is true about Him, even if your heart doesn't feel it at this moment.

Shirley Dobson

Let this be your chief object in prayer, to realize the presence of your heavenly Father. Let your watchword be: Alone with God.

Andrew Murray

A TIMELY TIP

Be still and listen to God. He has something important to say to you.

Chapter 18

I said a prayer for you today . . .
I prayed that you will
always serve God
with a humble heart.

Worship the Lord your God and . . .
serve Him only.

—

Matthew 4:10 HCSB

HUMBLE SERVICE

We live in a world that glorifies power, prestige, fame, and money. But the words of Jesus teach us that the most esteemed men and women in this world are not the self-congratulatory leaders of society but are instead the humblest of servants.

Are you willing to become a humble servant for Christ? Are you willing to pitch in and make the world a better place, or are you determined to keep all your blessings to yourself. The answers to these questions will determine the quantity and the quality of the service you render to God and to His children.

Today, you may feel the temptation to take more than you give. You may be tempted to withhold your generosity. Or you may be tempted to build yourself up in the eyes of your friends. Resist those temptations. Instead, serve your friends quietly and without fanfare. Find a need and fill it . . . humbly. Lend a helping hand . . . anonymously. As you go about your daily activities, remember that the Savior of all humanity made Himself a servant, and we, as His followers, must do no less.

MORE FROM GOD'S WORD

A person should consider us in this way: as servants of Christ and managers of God's mysteries. In this regard, it is expected of managers that each one be found faithful.

1 Corinthians 4:1-2 HCSB

If they serve Him obediently, they will end their days in prosperity and their years in happiness.

Job 36:11 HCSB

We must do the works of Him who sent Me while it is day. Night is coming when no one can work.

John 9:4 HCSB

Serve the Lord with gladness.

Psalm 100:2 HCSB

If anyone serves Me, let him follow Me; and where I am, there My servant will be also. If anyone serves Me, him My Father will honor.

John 12:26 NKJV

MORE GREAT IDEAS

In the very place where God has put us, whatever its limitations, whatever kind of work it may be, we may indeed serve the Lord Christ.

Elisabeth Elliot

Doing something positive toward another person is a practical approach to feeling good about yourself.

Barbara Johnson

Through our service to others, God wants to influence our world for Him.

Vonette Bright

If you want to discover your spiritual gifts, start obeying God. As you serve Him, you will find that He has given you the gifts that are necessary to follow through in obedience.

Anne Graham Lotz

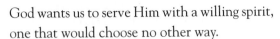

God wants us to serve Him with a willing spirit, one that would choose no other way.

Beth Moore

So many times we say that we can't serve God because we aren't whatever is needed. We're not talented enough or smart enough or whatever. But if you are in covenant with Jesus Christ, He is responsible for covering your weaknesses, for being your strength. He will give you His abilities for your disabilities!

Kay Arthur

God has lots of folks who intend to go to work for him "some day." What He needs is more people who are willing to work for Him today.

Marie T. Freeman

A TIMELY TIP

Jesus was a servant, and if you want to follow Him, you must be a servant, too—even when service requires sacrifice.

Chapter 19

I said a prayer for you today . . .
I prayed that you will
talk to God early and often.

*Be kindly affectionate to one another
with brotherly love, in honor giving preference
to one another; not lagging in diligence,
fervent in spirit, serving the Lord;
rejoicing in hope, patient in tribulation,
continuing steadfastly in prayer.*

—

Romans 12:10-12 NKJV

THE POWER OF PRAYER

"The power of prayer": these words are so familiar, yet sometimes we forget what they mean. Prayer is a powerful tool for communicating with our Creator; it is an opportunity to commune with the Giver of all things good. Prayer is not a thing to be taken lightly or to be used infrequently.

All too often, amid the rush of daily life, we may lose sight of God's presence in our lives. Instead of turning to Him for guidance and for comfort, we depend, instead, upon our own resources. To do so is a profound mistake. Prayer should never be reserved for mealtimes or for bedtimes; it should be an ever-present focus in our daily lives.

Today, instead of turning things over in our minds, let us turn them over to God in prayer. Instead of worrying about our decisions, let's trust God to help us make them. Today, let us pray constantly about things great and small. God is listening, and He wants to hear from us. Now.

MORE FROM GOD'S WORD

And everything—whatever you ask in prayer, believing—you will receive.

Matthew 21:22 HCSB

Rejoice always! Pray constantly. Give thanks in everything, for this is God's will for you in Christ Jesus.

1 Thessalonians 5:16-18 HCSB

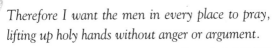

Therefore I want the men in every place to pray, lifting up holy hands without anger or argument.

1 Timothy 2:8 HCSB

The intense prayer of the righteous is very powerful.

James 5:16 HCSB

Yet He often withdrew to deserted places and prayed.

Luke 5:16 HCSB

101

MORE GREAT IDEAS

Your family and friends need your prayers and you need theirs. And God wants to hear those prayers. So what are you waiting for?

Marie T. Freeman

There is no way that Christians, in a private capacity, can do so much to promote the work of God and advance the kingdom of Christ as by prayer.

Jonathan Edwards

Prayer is never the least we can do; it is always the most!

A. W. Tozer

God knows that we, with our limited vision, don't even know that for which we should pray. When we entrust our requests to him, we trust him to honor our prayers with holy judgment.

Max Lucado

Prayer guards hearts and minds and causes God to bring peace out of chaos.

Beth Moore

Two wings are necessary to lift our souls toward God: prayer and praise. Prayer asks. Praise accepts the answer.

Mrs. Charles E. Cowman

Find a place to pray where no one imagines that you are praying. Then, shut the door and talk to God.

Oswald Chambers

A life growing in its purity and devotion will be a more prayerful life.

E. M. Bounds

A TIMELY TIP

Prayer changes things—and you—so pray.

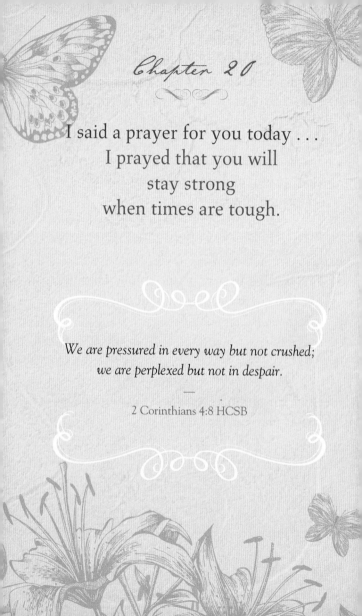

Chapter 20

I said a prayer for you today . . .
I prayed that you will
stay strong
when times are tough.

We are pressured in every way but not crushed;
we are perplexed but not in despair.

—

2 Corinthians 4:8 HCSB

ENDURING TOUGH TIMES

From time to time, all of us face adversity, discouragement, or disappointment. And, throughout life, we must all endure life-changing personal losses that leave us breathless. When we do, God stands ready to protect us. Psalm 147 promises, "He heals the brokenhearted, and binds their wounds" (v. 3 NIV).

When we are troubled, we must call upon God, and, in His own time and according to His own plan, He will heal us.

Are you anxious? Take those anxieties to God. Are you troubled? Take your troubles to Him. Does your world seem to be trembling beneath your feet? Seek protection from the One who cannot be moved. The same God who created the universe will protect you if you ask Him . . . so ask Him.

> Measure the size of the obstacles against the size of God.
>
> —
>
> Beth Moore

MORE FROM GOD'S WORD

I called to the Lord in my distress; I called to my God. From His temple He heard my voice.

2 Samuel 22:7 HCSB

I will be with you when you pass through the waters . . . when you walk through the fire . . . the flame will not burn you. For I the Lord your God, the Holy One of Israel, and your Savior.

Isaiah 43:2-3 HCSB

Consider it a great joy, my brothers, whenever you experience various trials, knowing that the testing of your faith produces endurance. But endurance must do its complete work, so that you may be mature and complete, lacking nothing.

James 1:2-4 HCSB

But as for you, you meant evil against me; but God meant it for good, in order to bring it about as it is this day, to save many people alive.

Genesis 50:20 NKJV

MORE GREAT IDEAS

God will never let you sink under your circumstances. He always provides a safety net and His love always encircles.

Barbara Johnson

If all struggles and sufferings were eliminated, the spirit would no more reach maturity than would the child.

Elisabeth Elliot

Faith is a strong power, mastering any difficulty in the strength of the Lord who made heaven and earth.

Corrie ten Boom

When problems threaten to engulf us, we must do what believers have always done, turn to the Lord for encouragement and solace. As Psalm 46:1 states, "God is our refuge and strength, an ever-present help in trouble."

Shirley Dobson

Even in the winter, even in the midst of the storm, the sun is still there. Somewhere, up above the clouds, it still shines and warms and pulls at the life buried deep inside the brown branches and frozen earth. The sun is there! Spring will come.

Gloria Gaither

God helps those who help themselves, but there are times when we are quite incapable of helping ourselves. That's when God stoops down and gathers us in His arms like a mother lifts a sick child, and does for us what we cannot do for ourselves.

Ruth Bell Graham

A TIMELY TIP

When times are tough, you should guard your heart by turning it over to God.

I said a prayer for you today . . .
I prayed that you will
treat each day
as a gift from God.

This is the day the LORD has made;
we will rejoice and be glad in it.

—

Psalm 118:24 NKJV

THIS IS THE DAY

The familiar words of Psalm 118:24 remind us of a profound yet simple truth: God created this day, and it's up to each of us to rejoice and to be grateful.

For Christian believers, every day begins and ends with God and His Son. Christ came to this earth to give us abundant life and eternal salvation. We give thanks to our Maker when we treasure each day and use it to the fullest.

This day is a gift from God. How will you use it? Will you celebrate God's gifts and obey His commandments? Will you share words of encouragement and hope with all who cross your path? Will you share the Good News of the risen Christ? Will you trust in the Father and praise His glorious handiwork? The answer to these questions will determine, to a surprising extent, the direction and the quality of your day.

So whatever this day holds for you, begin it and end it with God as your partner and Christ as your Savior. And throughout the day, give thanks to the One who created you and saved you. God's love for you is infinite. Accept it joyously and be thankful.

MORE FROM GOD'S WORD

I must work the works of Him who sent Me while it is day; the night is coming when no one can work.

John 9:4 NKJV

Therefore, get your minds ready for action, being self-disciplined, and set your hope completely on the grace to be brought to you at the revelation of Jesus Christ.

1 Peter 1:13 HCSB

Rejoice in the Lord always. I will say it again: Rejoice!

Philippians 4:4 HCSB

But encourage each other daily, while it is still called today, so that none of you is hardened by sin's deception.

Hebrews 3:13 HCSB

MORE GREAT IDEAS

Yesterday is the tomb of time, and tomorrow is the womb of time. Only now is yours.

R. G. Lee

Christ is the secret, the source, the substance, the center, and the circumference of all true and lasting gladness.

Mrs. Charles E. Cowman

When the dream of our heart is one that God has planted there, a strange happiness flows into us. At that moment, all of the spiritual resources of the universe are released to help us. Our praying is then at one with the will of God and becomes a channel for the Creator's purposes for us and our world.

Catherine Marshall

Submit each day to God, knowing that He is God over all your tomorrows.

Kay Arthur

If you can forgive the person you were, accept the person you are, and believe in the person you will become, you are headed for joy. So celebrate your life.

Barbara Johnson

If we are ever going to be or do anything for our Lord, now is the time.

Vance Havner

God gave you this glorious day. Don't disappoint Him. Use it for His glory.

Marie T. Freeman

A TIMELY TIP

When you celebrate God's gifts—when you place God's promises firmly in your mind and your heart—you'll find yourself celebrating life. And that, by the way, is exactly what God wants you to do.

Chapter 22

I said a prayer for you today . . .
I prayed that you will
keep things in
proper perspective.

Make your own attitude that of Christ Jesus.

—

Philippians 2:5 HCSB

MAINTAINING PERSPECTIVE

S ometimes, amid the demands of daily life, we lose perspective. Life seems out of balance, and the pressures of everyday living seem overwhelming. What's needed is a fresh perspective, a restored sense of balance . . . and God.

If a temporary loss of perspective has left you worried, exhausted, or both, it's time to readjust your thought patterns. Negative thoughts are habit-forming; thankfully, so are positive ones. With practice, you can form the habit of focusing on God's priorities and your possibilities. When you do, you'll soon discover that you will spend less time fretting about your challenges and more time praising God for His gifts.

When you call upon the Lord and prayerfully seek His will, He will give you wisdom and perspective. When you make God's priorities your priorities, He will direct your steps and calm your fears. So today and every day hereafter, pray for a sense of balance and perspective. And remember: your thoughts are intensely powerful things, so handle them with care.

MORE FROM GOD'S WORD

Let this mind be in you which was also in Christ Jesus, who, being in the form of God, did not consider it robbery to be equal with God, but made Himself of no reputation, taking the form of a bondservant, and coming in the likeness of men. And being found in appearance as a man, He humbled Himself and became obedient to the point of death, even the death of the cross.

Philippians 2:5-8 NKJV

Set your minds on what is above, not on what is on the earth.

Colossians 3:2 HCSB

For the word of God is living and powerful, and sharper than any two-edged sword, piercing even to the division of soul and spirit, and of joints and marrow, and is a discerner of the thoughts and intents of the heart.

Hebrews 4:12 NKJV

MORE GREAT IDEAS

Earthly fears are no fears at all. Answer the big questions of eternity, and the little questions of life fall into perspective.

Max Lucado

Instead of being frustrated and overwhelmed by all that is going on in our world, go to the Lord and ask Him to give you His eternal perspective.

Kay Arthur

Like a shadow declining swiftly . . . away . . . like the dew of the morning gone with the heat of the day; like the wind in the treetops, like a wave of the sea, so are our lives on earth when seen in light of eternity.

Ruth Bell Graham

Attitude is the mind's paintbrush; it can color any situation.

Barbara Johnson

117

The proper perspective creates within us a spirit of reaching outside of ourselves with joy and enthusiasm.

Luci Swindoll

What you see and hear depends a good deal on where you are standing; it also depends on what sort of person you are.

C. S. Lewis

Obey God one step at a time, then the next step will come into view.

Catherine Marshall

A TIMELY TIP

Keep things in perspective. Your life is an integral part of God's grand plan. So don't become unduly upset over the minor inconveniences of life, and don't worry too much about today's setbacks—they're temporary.

Chapter 23

I said a prayer for you today . . .
I prayed that you will accept
God's abundance.

I am come that they might have life,
and that they might have it more abundantly.

—

John 10:10 KJV

ACCEPTING GOD'S ABUNDANCE

The familiar words of John 10:10 should serve as a daily reminder: Christ came to this earth so that we might experience His abundance, His love, and His gift of eternal life. But Christ does not force Himself upon us; we must claim His gifts for ourselves.

Every woman knows that some days are so busy and so hurried that abundance seems a distant promise. It is not. Every day, we can claim the spiritual abundance that God promises for our lives . . . and we should.

Thomas Brooks spoke for believers of every generation when he observed, "Christ is the sun, and all the watches of our lives should be set by the dial of his motion." Christ, indeed, is the ultimate Savior of mankind and the personal Savior of those who believe in Him. As His servants, we should place Him at the very center of our lives. And, every day that God gives us breath, we should share Christ's love and His abundance with a world that needs both.

MORE FROM GOD'S WORD

Until now you have asked for nothing in My name. Ask and you will receive, that your joy may be complete.

John 16:24 HCSB

And God is able to make every grace overflow to you, so that in every way, always having everything you need, you may excel in every good work.

2 Corinthians 9:8 HCSB

My cup runs over. Surely goodness and mercy shall follow me all the days of my life; and I will dwell in the house of the Lord forever.

Psalm 23:5-6 NKJV

And He said to them, "Take heed and beware of covetousness, for one's life does not consist in the abundance of the things he possesses."

Luke 12:15 NKJV

MORE GREAT IDEAS

Yes, we were created for His holy pleasure, but we will ultimately—if not immediately—find much pleasure in His pleasure.

Beth Moore

It would be wrong to have a "poverty complex," for to think ourselves paupers is to deny either the King's riches or to deny our being His children.

Catherine Marshall

God's riches are beyond anything we could ask or even dare to imagine! If my life gets gooey and stale, I have no excuse.

Barbara Johnson

The gift of God is eternal life, spiritual life, abundant life through faith in Jesus Christ, the Living Word of God.

Anne Graham Lotz

God has promised us abundance, peace, and eternal life. These treasures are ours for the asking; all we must do is claim them. One of the great mysteries of life is why on earth do so many of us wait so very long to lay claim to God's gifts?

Marie T. Freeman

Get ready for God to show you not only His pleasure, but His approval.

Joni Eareckson Tada

God is the giver, and we are the receivers. And His richest gifts are bestowed not upon those who do the greatest things, but upon those who accept His abundance and His grace.

Hannah Whitall Smith

A TIMELY TIP

Don't miss out on God's abundance. Every day is a beautifully wrapped gift from God. Unwrap it; use it; and give thanks to the Giver.

Chapter 24

I said a prayer for you today . . .
I prayed that you will
discover your talents and
use them for God's glory.

Do not neglect the gift that is in you.

—

1 Timothy 4:14 HCSB

USING YOUR TALENTS

God gives each of us a unique assortment of talents and opportunities. And our Heavenly Father instructs us to be faithful stewards of the gifts that He bestows upon us. But we live in a world that encourages us to do otherwise.

Ours is a society that is filled to the brim with countless opportunities to squander our time, our resources, and our talents. So we must be watchful for distractions and temptations that might lead us astray.

God has blessed you with unique opportunities to serve Him, and He has given you every tool that you need to do so. Today, accept this challenge: value the talent that God has given you, nourish it, make it grow, and share it with the world. After all, the best way to say "Thank You" for God's gifts is to use them.

> You are the only person on earth who can use your ability.
>
> —
>
> Zig Ziglar

MORE FROM GOD'S WORD

So he who had received five talents came and brought five other talents, saying, "Lord, you delivered to me five talents; look, I have gained five more talents besides them." His lord said to him, "Well done, good and faithful servant; you were faithful over a few things, I will make you ruler over many things. Enter into the joy of your lord."

Matthew 25:20-21 NKJV

Each one has his own gift from God, one in this manner and another in that.

1 Corinthians 7:7 NKJV

I remind you to keep ablaze the gift of God that is in you.

2 Timothy 1:6 HCSB

Based on the gift they have received, everyone should use it to serve others, as good managers of the varied grace of God.

1 Peter 4:10 HCSB

MORE GREAT IDEAS

If you want to reach your potential, you need to add a strong work ethic to your talent.

John Maxwell

Not everyone possesses boundless energy or a conspicuous talent. We are not equally blessed with great intellect or physical beauty or emotional strength. But we have all been given the same ability to be faithful.

Gigi Graham Tchividjian

God often reveals His direction for our lives through the way He made us . . . with a certain personality and unique skills.

Bill Hybels

You are a unique blend of talents, skills, and gifts, which makes you an indispensable member of the body of Christ.

Charles Stanley

In the great orchestra we call life, you have an instrument and a song, and you owe it to God to play them both sublimely.

Max Lucado

Employ whatever God has entrusted you with, in doing good, all possible good, in every possible kind and degree.

John Wesley

Discipline is the refining fire by which talent becomes ability.

Roy L. Smith

God has given you special talents—now it's your turn to give them back to God.

Marie T. Freeman

A TIMELY TIP

God has given you a unique array of talents and opportunities. The rest is up to you.

I said a prayer for you today . . .
I prayed that you will be
a good example
for others to follow.

You should be an example to the believers
in speech, in conduct, in love,
in faith, in purity.

—

1 Timothy 4:12 HCSB

THE RIGHT KIND OF EXAMPLE

What kind of example are you? Are you the kind of person whose life serves as a powerful example of decency and morality? Are you a person whose behavior serves as a positive role model for others? Are you the kind of person whose actions, day in and day out, are based upon integrity, fidelity, and a love for the Lord? If so, you are not only blessed by God, but you are also a powerful force for good in a world that desperately needs positive influences such as yours.

We live in a dangerous, temptation-filled world. That's why you encounter so many opportunities to stray from God's commandments. Resist those temptations! When you do, you'll earn God's blessings and you'll serve as a positive role model for your family and friends.

Phillips Brooks advised, "Be such a man, and live such a life, that if every man were such as you, and every life a life like yours, this earth would be God's Paradise." And that's sound advice because our families and friends are watching . . . and so, for that matter, is God.

MORE FROM GOD'S WORD

Do everything without grumbling and arguing, so that you may be blameless and pure.

Philippians 2:14-15 HCSB

Set an example of good works yourself, with integrity and dignity in your teaching.

Titus 2:7 HCSB

For the kingdom of God is not in talk but in power.

1 Corinthians 4:20 HCSB

Therefore since we also have such a large cloud of witnesses surrounding us, let us lay aside every weight and the sin that so easily ensnares us, and run with endurance the race that lies before us.

Hebrews 12:1 HCSB

You are the light of the world. A city situated on a hill cannot be hidden.

Matthew 5:14 HCSB

MORE GREAT IDEAS

Heredity does not equip a child with proper attitudes; children learn what they are taught. We cannot expect proper behavior to appear magically.

James Dobson

A true mother is not merely a provider, housekeeper, comforter, or companion. A true mother is primarily and essentially a trainer.

Ruth Bell Graham

If you want your neighbor to know what Christ will do for him, let the neighbor see what Christ has done for you.

Henry Ward Beecher

Whether we signed up for the responsibility or not, Christian parents give their children impressions of what they can expect from God.

Beth Moore

Living life with a consistent spiritual walk deeply influences those we love most.

Vonette Bright

Mothers must model the tenderness we need. Our world can't find it anywhere else.

Charles Swindoll

We must mirror God's love in the midst of a world full of hatred. We are the mirrors of God's love, so we may show Jesus by our lives.

Corrie ten Boom

A TIMELY TIP

As a Christian, the most important light you shine is the light that your own life shines on the lives of others. May your light shine brightly, righteously, obediently, and eternally!

Chapter 26

I said a prayer for you today . . .
I prayed that you will
work hard and that your
hard work will be rewarded.

Whatever you do, do it enthusiastically,
as something done for the Lord
and not for men.

—

Colossians 3:23 HCSB

THE REWARDS OF HARD WORK

The old adage is both familiar and true: We must pray as if everything depended upon God, but work as if everything depended upon us. Yet sometimes, when we are weary and discouraged, we may allow our worries to sap our energy and our hope. God has other intentions. God intends that we pray for things, and He intends that we be willing to work for the things that we pray for. More importantly, God intends that our work should become His work.

> Few things fire up a person's commitment like dedication to excellence.
>
> —
>
> John Maxwell

Are you willing to work diligently for yourself and for your God? And are you willing to engage in work that is pleasing to your Creator? If so, you can expect your Heavenly Father to bring forth a rich harvest.

MORE FROM GOD'S WORD

He did it with all his heart. So he prospered.

2 Chronicles 31:21 NKJV

Whatever your hands find to do, do with [all] your strength.

Ecclesiastes 9:10 HCSB

Don't work only while being watched, in order to please men, but as slaves of Christ, do God's will from your heart. Render service with a good attitude, as to the Lord and not to men.

Ephesians 6:6-7 HCSB

We must do the works of Him who sent Me while it is day. Night is coming when no one can work.

John 9:4 HCSB

The people had a mind to work.

Nehemiah 4:6 KJV

MORE GREAT IDEAS

Ordinary work, which is what most of us do most of the time, is ordained by God every bit as much as is the extraordinary.

Elisabeth Elliot

You can't climb the ladder of life with your hands in your pockets.

Barbara Johnson

Great relief and satisfaction can come from seeking God's priorities for us in each season, discerning what is "best" in the midst of many noble opportunities, and pouring our most excellent energies into those things.

Beth Moore

Thank God every morning when you get up that you have something which must be done, whether you like it or not. Work breeds a hundred virtues that idleness never knows.

Charles Kingsley

In the very place where God has put us, whatever its limitations, whatever kind of work it may be, we may indeed serve the Lord Christ.

Elisabeth Elliot

If you honor God with your work, He will honor you because of your work.

Marie T. Freeman

It may be that the day of judgment will dawn tomorrow; in that case, we shall gladly stop working for a better tomorrow. But not before.

Dietrich Bonhoeffer

A TIMELY TIP

Here's a time-tested formula for success: have faith in God and do the work. It has been said that there are no shortcuts to any place worth going. Hard work is not simply a proven way to get ahead, it's also part of God's plan for all His children (including you).

I said a prayer for you today . . .
I prayed that you will
turn all your worries
over to God.

*Don't worry about your life, what you will eat
or what you will drink; or about your body,
what you will wear. Isn't life more than food
and the body more than clothing?*

—

Matthew 6:25 HCSB

BEYOND WORRY

Here's a riddle: What is it that is too unimportant to pray about yet too big for God to handle? The answer, of course, is: "nothing." Yet sometimes, when the challenges of the day seem overwhelming, we may spend more time worrying about our troubles than praying about them. And, we may spend more time fretting about our problems than solving them. A far better strategy is to pray as if everything depended entirely upon God and to work as if everything depended entirely upon us.

What we see as problems God sees as opportunities. And if we are to trust Him completely, we must acknowledge that even when our own vision is dreadfully impaired, His vision is perfect.

Today and every day, let us trust God by courageously confronting the things that we see as problems and He sees as possibilities. And while we're at it, let's remind our friends and family members that no problem is too big for God . . . not even our problems.

MORE FROM GOD'S WORD

Don't worry about anything, but in everything, through prayer and petition with thanksgiving, let your requests be made known to God.

Philippians 4:6 HCSB

Therefore don't worry about tomorrow, because tomorrow will worry about itself. Each day has enough trouble of its own.

Matthew 6:34 HCSB

Yea, though I walk through the valley of the shadow of death, I will fear no evil: for thou art with me; thy rod and thy staff they comfort me.

Psalm 23:4 KJV

I will be with you when you pass through the waters . . . when you walk through the fire . . . the flame will not burn you. For I the Lord your God, the Holy One of Israel, and your Savior.

Isaiah 43:2-3 HCSB

MORE GREAT IDEAS

Today is mine. Tomorrow is none of my business. If I peer anxiously into the fog of the future, I will strain my spiritual eyes so that I will not see clearly what is required of me now.

Elisabeth Elliott

We are not called to be burden-bearers, but cross-bearers and light-bearers. We must cast our burdens on the Lord.

Corrie ten Boom

Worry is the senseless process of cluttering up tomorrow's opportunities with leftover problems from today.

Barbara Johnson

Never yield to gloomy anticipation. Place your hope and confidence in God. He has no record of failure.

Mrs. Charles E. Cowman

Anxiety may be natural and normal for the world, but it is not to be part of a believer's lifestyle.

Kay Arthur

Walk by faith! Stop the plague of worry. Relax! Learn to say, "Lord, this is Your battle."

Charles Swindoll

This life of faith, then, consists in just this—being a child in the Father's house. Let the ways of childish confidence and freedom from care, which so please you and win your heart when you observe your own little ones, teach you what you should be in your attitude toward God.

Hannah Whitall Smith

A TIMELY TIP

An important part of becoming a more mature Christian is learning to worry less and to trust God more.

Chapter 28

I said a prayer for you today . . .
I prayed that you will
never lose faith
in your own abilities.

For You have made him a little lower than
the angels, and You have crowned him
with glory and honor.

—

Psalm 8:5 NKJV

BELIEVE IN YOURSELF!

D o you believe that you deserve the best, and that you can achieve the best? Or have you convinced yourself that you're a second-tier talent who'll be lucky to finish far back in the pack? Before you answer that question, remember this: God sent His Son so that you might enjoy the abundant life that Jesus describes in the familiar words of John 10:10. But, God's gifts are not guaranteed—it's up to you to claim them.

As you plan for the next stage of your life's journey, promise yourself that when it comes to the important things in life, you won't settle for second best. And what, pray tell, are the "important things"? Your faith, your family, your health, and your relationships, for starters. In each of these areas, you deserve to be a rip-roaring, top-drawer success.

So if you want to achieve the best that life has to offer, convince yourself that you have the ability to earn all the rewards that God has in store for you. Become sold on yourself—sold on your opportunities, sold on your potential, sold on your abilities. If you're sold on yourself, chances are the world will soon become sold, too, and the results will be beautiful.

MORE FROM GOD'S WORD

How happy are those whose way is blameless, who live according to the law of the Lord! Happy are those who keep His decrees and seek Him with all their heart.

Psalm 119:1-2 HCSB

Happy is the one whose help is the God of Jacob, whose hope is in the Lord his God.

Psalm 146:5 HCSB

If God is for us, who is against us?

Romans 8:31 HCSB

For it was You who created my inward parts; You knit me together in my mother's womb. I will praise You, because I have been remarkably and wonderfully made. Your works are wonderful, and I know [this] very well.

Psalm 139:13-14 HCSB

MORE GREAT IDEAS

When it comes to our position before God, we're perfect. When he sees each of us, he sees one who has been made perfect through the One who is perfect—Jesus Christ.

Max Lucado

Being loved by Him whose opinion matters most gives us the security to risk loving, too—even loving ourselves.

Gloria Gaither

Give yourself a gift today: be present with yourself. God is. Enjoy your own personality. God does.

Barbara Johnson

The Creator has made us each one of a kind. There is nobody else exactly like us, and there never will be. Each of us is his special creation and is alive for a distinctive purpose.

Luci Swindoll

Comparison is the root of all feelings of inferiority.

James Dobson

Once you loosen up, let yourself be who you are: the wonderful, witty woman whom God will use to encourage and uplift other people.

Barbara Johnson

I was learning something important: we are most vulnerable to the piercing winds of doubt when we distance ourselves from the mission and fellowship to which Christ has called us. Our night of discouragement will seem endless and our task impossible, unless we recognize that He stands in our midst.

Joni Eareckson Tada

A TIMELY TIP

Old-fashioned respect never goes out of style—respect for other people and respect for the person in the mirror.

I said a prayer for you today . . .
I prayed that you will
never lose your enthusiasm
for life.

He did it with all his heart. So he prospered.

—

2 Chronicles 31:21 NKJV

ENTHUSIASM FOR THE JOURNEY

Can you truthfully say that you are an enthusiastic person? Are you passionate about your faith, your life, your family, and your future? Hopefully so. But if your zest for life has waned, it is now time to redirect your efforts and recharge your spiritual batteries. And that means refocusing your priorities by putting God first.

Each day is a glorious opportunity to serve God and to do His will. Are you enthused about life, or do you struggle through each day giving scarcely a thought to God's blessings? Are you constantly praising God for His gifts, and are you sharing His Good News with the world? You should be.

Nothing is more important than your wholehearted commitment to God and to His only begotten Son. Your faith must never be an afterthought; it must be your ultimate priority, your ultimate possession, and your ultimate passion. When you become passionate about your faith, you'll become passionate about your life, too.

MORE FROM GOD'S WORD

I have seen that there is nothing better than for a person to enjoy his activities, because that is his reward. For who can enable him to see what will happen after he dies?

Ecclesiastes 3:22 HCSB

Do not lack diligence; be fervent in spirit; serve the Lord.

Romans 12:11 HCSB

Whatever you do, do it enthusiastically, as something done for the Lord and not for men.

Colossians 3:23 HCSB

This is the day the Lord has made; let us rejoice and be glad in it.

Psalm 118:24 HCSB

Render service with a good attitude, as to the Lord and not to men.

Ephesians 6:7 HCSB

MORE GREAT IDEAS

Enthusiasm, like the flu, is contagious—we get it from one another.

Barbara Johnson

We urgently need people who encourage and inspire us to move toward God and away from the world's enticing pleasures.

Jim Cymbala

Wouldn't it make an astounding difference, not only in the quality of the work we do, but also in the satisfaction, even our joy, if we recognized God's gracious gift in every single task?

Elisabeth Elliot

God is the giver, and we are the receivers. And His richest gifts are bestowed not upon those who do the greatest things, but upon those who accept His abundance and His grace.

Hannah Whitall Smith

Making up a string of excuses is usually harder than doing the work.

Marie T. Freeman

I don't know about you, but I want to do more than survive life—I want to mount up like the eagle and glide over rocky crags, nest in the tallest of trees, dive for nourishment in the deepest of mountain lakes, and soar on the wings of the wind.

Barbara Johnson

Your light is the truth of the Gospel message itself as well as your witness as to Who Jesus is and what He has done for you. Don't hide it.

Anne Graham Lotz

A TIMELY TIP

Don't wait for enthusiasm to find you, go looking for it. Look at your life and your relationships as exciting adventures.

Chapter 30

I said a prayer for you today . . .
I prayed that you will always
worship God
with a sincere heart.

*But an hour is coming, and is now here,
when the true worshipers will worship the Father
in spirit and truth. Yes, the Father wants such
people to worship Him. God is Spirit,
and those who worship Him must worship
in spirit and truth.*

—

John 4:23-24 HCSB

THE IMPORTANCE OF WORSHIP

All of humanity is engaged in worship. The question is not whether we worship, but what we worship. Wise men and women choose to worship God. When they do, they are blessed with a plentiful harvest of joy, peace, and abundance. Other people choose to distance themselves from God by foolishly worshiping things that are intended to bring personal gratification but not spiritual gratification. Such choices often have tragic consequences.

If we place our love for material possessions above our love for God—or if we yield to the countless temptations of this world—we find ourselves engaged in a struggle between good and evil, a clash between God and Satan. Our responses to these struggles have implications that echo throughout our families and throughout our communities.

How can we ensure that we cast our lot with God? We do so, in part, by the practice of regular, purposeful worship in the company of fellow believers. When we worship God faithfully and fervently, we are blessed. When we fail to worship God, for whatever reason, we forfeit the spiritual gifts that He intends for us.

We must worship our Heavenly Father, not just with our words, but also with deeds. We must honor Him, praise Him, and obey Him. As we seek to find purpose and meaning for our lives, we must first seek His purpose and His will. For believers, God comes first. Always first.

Praise Him!
Praise Him!
Tell of His excellent greatness.
Praise Him!
Praise Him!
Ever in joyful song!

—

Fanny Crosby

MORE FROM GOD'S WORD

So that at the name of Jesus every knee should bow—of those who are in heaven and on earth and under the earth—and every tongue should confess that Jesus Christ is Lord, to the glory of God the Father.

Philippians 2:10-11 HCSB

If anyone is thirsty, he should come to Me and drink!

John 7:37 HCSB

And every day they devoted themselves to meeting together in the temple complex, and broke bread from house to house. They ate their food with gladness and simplicity of heart, praising God and having favor with all the people. And every day the Lord added those being saved to them.

Acts 2:46-47 HCSB

I rejoiced with those who said to me, "Let us go to the house of the Lord."

Psalm 122:1 HCSB

MORE GREAT IDEAS

God asks that we worship Him with our concentrated minds as well as with our wills and emotions. A divided and scattered mind is not effective.

Catherine Marshall

Spiritual worship comes from our very core and is fueled by an awesome reverence and desire for God.

Beth Moore

To worship Him in truth means to worship Him honestly, without hypocrisy, standing open and transparent before Him.

Anne Graham Lotz

Worship is spiritual. Our worship must be more than just outward expression, it must also take place in our spirits.

Franklin Graham

God actually delights in and pursues our worship (Proverbs 15:8 & John 4:23).

Shirley Dobson

In the sanctuary, we discover beauty: the beauty of His presence.

Kay Arthur

Worship and worry cannot live in the same heart; they are mutually exclusive.

Ruth Bell Graham

God has promised to give you all of eternity. The least you can do is give Him one day a week in return.

Marie T. Freeman

A TIMELY TIP

The best way to worship God . . . is to worship Him sincerely and often.